THERE'S SOMETHING THEY'RE NOT TELLING US

ALSO BY KIMBERLY KRUGE

Ordinary Chaos

THERE'S SOMETHING THEY'RE NOT TELLING US

KIMBERLY KRUGE

Carnegie Mellon University Press
Pittsburgh 2022

ACKNOWLEDGMENTS

Grateful acknowledgment is made to the editors of the journals in which versions of the following poems also appeared:

AGNI: "Garden," "Two Ways"; *Connotation Press: An Online Artifact*: "On Having Children," "Terminal," "Undesirable Thoughts"; *The Hopkins Review*: "Swimming"; *Negative Capability Press* (web feature): "Prayer"; *The Missouri Review* (poem of the day, online): "Living, An Epigraph"; *Ploughshares*: "San Sebastián"

I would like to thank the Millay Colony for the Arts for providing the time and space in which to write, revise, and order poems herein. I would similarly like to thank the owners of the studio in Bosque de La Primavera that I rent, and in which I've brought this and other manuscripts to completion.

Many thanks to those who have been my mentors, readers, and steadfast supporters, especially: Cleopatra Mathis and the the creative writing department at Dartmouth College; Heather McHugh, Martha Rhodes, Stephen Dobyns, Connie Voisine, Bruce Coffin, Rick Barot, Gabrielle Calvocoressi, and the professors and staff of the Warren Wilson Writing MFA Program; Alexia Halteman, Carlos Armenta, and the late José Clemente Orozco of Impronta Casa Editora.

Especially grateful for my family: my parents, Anthony and Jennifer Kruge; and my sister Rebecca, and her family: her husband, Travis, and their children, Jude and Cora.

Thank you to the following people for being part of my life for many years and allowing me to support them as humans and artists: Gabriella Collins-Fernandez and family, Jennifer Hart, Tessa Murphy, Christianne Dawis, Miesha Smith, Fiona Lundie and family, and Zack Styskal and Corey Goodman.

Special thanks to the incredibly wise, quick-witted, and inspiring souls of Comala Haven 2017, 2018, 2019, 2020, and 2021. I'd especially like to thank Carrie Mar, Claudia Rangel, Amy Lin, Leigh Lucas, Taryn Tilton, Avra Elliott, Katherine Rooks, and Esme Franklin.

Additional thanks to Amy Lin for offering up brilliant suggestions to solidify the format of several poems of this book and for her patient feedback; also, to Taryn Tilton, Leigh Lucas, Avra Elliott, and Katherine Rooks for their keen recommendations on ordering and formatting the poems herein.

To the members of my Warren Wilson cohort who have kindly continued to support my work and projects: Jennifer Funk, Jennifer Büchi, Rebecca Lund, Nathan McClain, Kaisa Edy, Geoff Kronik, Rolf Yngve, Brent Walth, Eilis Maynard, and the aforementioned women of Comala Haven.

Book design by Amber Quinn

for Cora and Jude

CONTENTS

LIVING, AN EPIGRAPH

All I have ever wanted in this life is to live,
        but our ghosts all day climb and descend the stairs.

When you sleep, I must shake you awake at least
        three times, monitor the rise and fall of your abdomen.

When the dog sleeps I must do the same.
        Every morning I wonder why we planted

a tree with ephemeral blooms, and I mourn
        what has been devoured by our industrious ants.

When did all this start? This absence of living?
        I found a note I'd written to myself that said

make a list combining all other lists. It would seem
        I actually thought I might do this,

but instead   I starved   I ran on limp legs
        I drank   I yanked out my hair   I stopped listening for

the voice of reason:
        the piecewise drop of the forest's canopy

the click of the door
        the shuffle of light across

the floor and our steps on it
        everywhere occasioning the din of shadow

O

TWO WAYS

The night before my mother stopped working, we walked
the pier, and the crane effected geometric deaths on the bluefish—
work more perfect than a knife's. The night was sharp

and we were soft, talking about tides and the people who are always
at every juncture. Sometimes you can walk the sandbar to the middle
of the sea and sometimes you can't. If you had all the money in the world

which house would you buy? We both choose the same one with a wraparound
body and an intimidating hearth. I want to say to her *mother for me there are two ways
to stop doing anything*. One is to be the lone, lazy fisherwoman at the end of the

jetty, waiting for my fish to come in, each wave listlessly toppling another
until it makes me sick to my stomach to watch them. The other way is to
walk straight into the sea roused by just how cold it is and how lost I am—

the water filling my eardrums with a deafening sustained note.
I'd think myself a genius for this symphony; you know I would.
Instead I say *mother the crane is a glutton and a slob,*

on his sixth fish, blood browning the tide pools and bones strewn.
Heads. Tails. It's too much for her. Either too excessive or ridiculous,
but I can't tell which. She is walking away, getting distance from me,

loving me still but with exasperation and an upward tilt of the head.
—How lost I am—I follow her home, a step behind her and her thoughts which are
many steps ahead: locking the door for the night, setting an alarm and keeping on.

QUIZ: HOW APATHETIC ARE YOU?

Did you know that apathy was originally considered a good thing? Apathy meaning indifference, freedom, passionless existence. By this definition, how apathetic are you? What did it mean to you when the tether between you and the other started to loosen and the other lifted up off the ground and out of the house, through the strategic but often overlooked skylight you chose to build; when the other began to keep secrets like foil wrappers and extra liters of water bought in a panic at the pharmacy? And when he kept other secrets like never finishing the last chapters of books? Doing things but not truly doing them: watering the ferns in the most drawn out mimetism possible or bearing towards you, the lover, then the wife, so imperceptibly in bed that not even the air could change in the room. Would you have noticed? Is it possible you believe the mountain has one long season? Tell us: do you think it is similar to not check the brakes on the car and not notice now how the vegetation changes from coniferous to scrub to semi-deciduous to mangrove along the highway? Because you used to care about that trajectory, thought even that it had worth, and you could feel its worth heating your chest and swelling the ducts of your eyes. You used to cry. Remember? You used to not check gas lines for a reason. Because you were going to live *pase lo que pase*. And events would come to pass and you would take them in, hold them in your gut, and grind them in your joints. You were once so sad that you lit your life on fire like the swailing of a field, and you waited for new roots to take; you thought, now this will be my Eden, garden of indifference and fat fruit. Did it work? Have you achieved apathy? What are you waiting for? Find out.

COMALA

I am going to explain to myself how to write about love and lovers. Leave out the
    grandiose valley

and the poor sheep you're dying to include. Smother the chit-chat and light the
    canopy on fire. Focus

on the molding between the boulders of the walls, on the tepid shower head; no, not
    on the Ugly,

not on the Real; on how since this is the eighth time or so your lover's stopped
    gauging how much

you might want it. Focus on the uncomplicated dinner and diet soda you enjoyed so
    heartily,

on the waiter with parted hair and a good disposition. Where is the volcano? The
    waiter answers,

it's right there. It's literally right there. This is what I'm getting at: if the cloud cover
    is thick enough

you can't even see 11,000 feet of volcano. How badly we want to be on fire. We drive
    in circles, idiots

and lovers, pointing, saying, is that fire, is it? Don't write about the lava or the
    absence of lava;

write about being out there prowling the crater. You can't imagine how badly it wants

rain. It's the ninth time, tenth time, a movie on a fuzzy screen. Does your lover know
there are

those who call static rain? You may not be able to see the volcano but you sure can
hear it,

and when you hear it you'll know whether it's about to love you or destroy you. Don't
you dare

write about the destruction. Foolish woman. Write about the love. This is a love
poem after all.

Producto [product / outlines / marriage / the space between bodies at an altar, *Lord I said I would never* until I was trimming his hair with the kitchen shears on the wash patio telling him how good he'd look on a street in Vienna, London, Barcelona, until he was on his way and the absence sat on everything, from the spoils on the fruit to the patio to the avenue, all the way down to the farthest street I knew the name of in Guadalajara, that street where everything is sold for parts]

Usos relevantes [relevant uses / what is it for / what does it do / it is, marriage, for making the bed because making the bed is sane, it is for spraying against insects, it is for shaking out the vines latched to the fence and exposing the nest and saying Look here was good enough for some creature to mate]

Urgencias [Emergencies, the state of, Please Call, urgently, a cord stretched across seas, across continents, across our room, I just had to tell you, Did you know, What were you thinking, Today I saw, This is what it is, No it isn't that at all]

Clasificación de la sustancia [Classification of the substance, nomenclature, naming, giving out words, another poet said that to say he loved his wife was to say it was getting late, was to ask if she knew how to drive, I say it is to forget the milk, I say it is to give names to rocks, I say it is to see a color and say That color is and invent a word for the blank]

FAMILY

When I married I had to separate the grains of salt of men and man.
Hold me, said man. Hold me, I replied. And so, history hushed itself out.
On the day of a family funeral, I instead took man to the museum to cry,
to implore Caravaggio about what it's like to send one's own head off
for absolution. And, man opened his hands as if to cradle a tender object—
see it there: redemption vacillating between two kinks in a strand.

INTERROGATION:

Are you yesterday's self? You whom I have
the most difficulty addressing? Metal bands
clanging on rough-boned hands. Body in seams.
Rucksack eyes. Gnarled spine. I don't mean
to offend. A version of you was so lovely that having
walked a mile in the rain to the newsstand, you
made another body exclaim. So wet! So beautiful!

Conv.   THE WINDOW

Wife & Husband

Our first night in the suburbs my husband asks where would you hide
in the case of a drive-by   I immediately say the downstairs bathroom   yes
the downstairs bathroom is good   he says   my brother and I were experts
at this game   every new place we lived   where would you hide if bullets
started to fly and yes the downstairs bathroom is good because
it has only one window small and high though that will never   though
never say never because then one says never and
but nothing ever happens this close to nature

VIOLIN SPIDER

Its eyes and markings rupture against the wall;
backhand and a boot. I have become an exterminator. Godspeed
to you whose hand is in the cranny grasping
for shears. If you are not bitten, then cut me down
a pomegranate. I want words like wanting meat.
Pericarp, aril, and mesocarp in my teeth.

QUIZ: HOW RESILIENT ARE YOU?

How able are you to face pain and hardship? Do you remember the time you scrapped the barren field and flew off? Your mother's voice now always on the line with the resonance of the wind of her walk. Croaks of familial knowing in a balmy exchange across the long thicket of the Americas. What a range of wild life. What a byzantine path. How is it that you or anyone can tolerate the implications of any one choice over another? This sounds very technical, but what it means is: how is it that you tolerate choosing to be in a place? Canning up the voices on the line and sealing them off. Are you absent? Or is it all happening in the in-between? We may be striking a nerve; here is pain. You wanted to see your sister's child make an "o" out of his mouth and the tenderness thicken like a vine in this woman you've always known. You wanted to pour your mother's water. Clean the crumbs from your father's desk as a gesture. Do you recall the ways you used to show love? Repainting a wall? Love-showing is mostly about work. Could you tolerate not doing this work? We've seen you line up the heels of shoes and square the corners of books. We've seen you put out food enough. We hear you calling night after night. We know you'll go to them. *Tranquila*, it is all happening in the in-between, in the long thicket, in the night thick with balm. *Calma*, you can be in two places at once. How could anyone tolerate space otherwise? How could we ever take our hand off of one pulse in order to count out another? Do you want to measure how much you can take? Start in on it.

SWIMMING

If I drop this into the deep,
    will you dive down and retrieve it for me?

My mother, at the community pool, a diadem
    of false pearls in her hair, is up to her shoulders in water.

It depends on how.
    You know I'd.

I will get lost. My face so
    different from the day before.

My legs unrecognizably damaged.
    It is all happening at an alarming rate:

loss. Somewhere between a lucid state
    and one that is elsewhere,

I envision that my tendons
    separate from the bones.

How will I tread water now?
    Right below the surface is

a thought I've just dropped.
    I don't even try. Mother:

everything is happening now
    at an alarming rate. Why

couldn't I save myself
    from becoming deteriorated,

from watching as my
    mind was dragged down

beyond reach. I can still see it there,
    but I don't know what it looks like—

does that make sense to you?
    I would like to be able—

I'd grasp the frail band fallen
    from your hair, if I weren't so sorry for myself.

Last night I forgot to make you dinner,
    and when I looked over at the table

there you were with water and
    a peanut butter sandwich.

I could still see you there,
    but I couldn't tell what you looked like,

and you could tell that I was there,
    watching you, but you couldn't

see me. Does that make sense
    to anyone? I had never felt

so much anguish as I did then;
    I used to know you, and you me,

but I understand it now: too much
    of a good thing; too much life;

too much creation; hypoxia;
    oversimplification. We are

becoming nothing; it is not
    the other way around.

I have to let this thought go
    or it will kill me, but

the thought will get away
    either way and still kill me.

It will steal itself from me and steal
    the feeling of the dear way I held onto it too.

Mother, I don't think we keep our crowns.
    We don't even keep our heads.

Elementos de la etiqueta [Label elements / what we are and where we are headed, the river is coming undone at the seams, the forest is ablaze, I am having a season of *Deslizamiento*, he is having a season of *Deslizamiento*, we saw the phenomenon of a green flash silently boom out from the horizon line before the sun imploded into the sea and it worked like a cut between two versions of our lives, spliced, before and after, before we soaked our hair in the salt, after we dried our hair in the dark]

Mezclas [Mixtures / to give order and morph, four Decembers and I do not remember but one, I cut my thigh on the rusted nail that held tight the curtain just to one side of the bathroom in which on one of those other Decembers we bathed solely with water from a bucket, awoke our skin and shocked our scalps and went our ways and always came back]

Otros peligros [Other dangers / risks, in no specific order: utterances, theft, deluges, scrapes, water, standing, burns, letting the dog off the leash, fire, drowning, failure, *narcobloqueos*, hitmen, bands of wild horses, heavy trunks, organ damage, chemical fertilizer, Is the fruit edible or is it not, Ask the dog, unresolved questions, coins, handshakes, sex, altitude, loss, Is the snake venomous or is it not, Ask the Internet, doubt, what are we and where are we headed, the house is coming undone at the junctures, see appendix]

MALOS PASOS

This morning, I took my death for a walk.

I desired the barbed-wire fence around the lot for sale,
extrapolated the divine sequence of a weed. Thistle nodded. Men
whistled and leered. I reached into my pocket, a wistful sag. Felt
for coins. What is survival if not just being low on
the triage of tragedy? I'll spend my tender on a crawling plant, guide it
up the house in a final act. What I've learned about *tragedy*
is that it is a word without precedent. Created expressly
to describe work that won't turn out right, and that for this
humans have a need. Your vine will devour you. Try to write
someone else's tragedy. They are not your incantations.
It is not your vigilant candle prodding the air of the house.
The grief destined for you loiters in your curtains.

I cradled the plant home and opened up the ground.

THE KNIFE

Husband & Brother

Brother   grandfather went to kill his lover's lover   he grabbed the knife
he went there walking   Brother I'm not exaggerating wish I could say
he ran   wish I could say he had a sentence in mind   wish
I could say he went through with it   but Brother   he turned around
this he did for us   congested rough-brained boys   Brother
another thing last night I couldn't sleep   a rat in the wall
startling and retreating   if only I could have found it
but it's still here   Brother   Brother   do you hear me   can you hear it

INTERROGATION:

I have never seen you. Or, have I
seen you too many ways? A lightweight shook out
at the ring. Accepting a bite into a your supple thigh.
Cracked and dried with lack. Branches of ephemera:
one bud flush, one a dropper. At your prime, a stranger
chased you forty blocks in the night with a snatched
bouquet and you outran both stranger and self.

INTERRUPTION

My mind was not here.
    I was beneath the loose, wet earth of something I'd read,
        making symbols as a *Homo Neanderthalensis.*

I was reading about myself on the wall
    of the anthropology museum in Mexico City,
        and eating a raw potato from a field in Belarus,

hearing the sound barrier broken by a Russian jet. I was on
    a bad transatlantic flight. I was worried about the engine.
        I was hiding in the woods from my mother,

the yellow light of the house in squares and satellites circling.
    I was looking down at earth, watching the plates shift and ram,
        and I was in bed on the sixth floor of someone else's building

listening to the news saying we'd all be alright as the city undulated.
    I was worried about the gas lines. About poisoning. I was thinking
        in my mother tongue. I hope it's all about more than it appears:

obscure tools and weekends, inventions of work and of rest.
    A man is at the door. A man knocks. This isn't up to me.
    He'll come in whether I want him or not.

WHEN DID IT START

Wife & Therapist

I had gone to town   I had an acronym   I forgot the Bread, the Water   unbelievable
        that despite the circumstance of the world
there had been a carnival   belts and wingtips   bacchanal under a swarm
        of flies   pig's leg   sheep's head   tripe
found myself in an alley between a Ferris wheel and a military van   boys rockabye-ing
        guns on their laps   boys masked to the eyes
having a dirty thought   a woman inverted   stacked masa in a mound   a plant
        wept off a balcony
a stray followed another stray down an alley   I think it was there   on the tail of a dog
        retreating   that I thought I may be
the last woman of humanity   does that make sense   I remembered life   us women
        warming our hair in the sun   and now
I am lucky if I   am I explaining myself   I am pursued   it's these fast legs   this skin
        pliant brain   mane enough to weave

General [Overview, bird's eye, mind's, body's, work across the sheets, say It's better with you, hold each other practically to death and fall asleep to the spiral crowing of a bird, lizard, insect we cannot see and therefore not define, not a tree in earshot of the bedroom window, but it is still out there crowing, demanding, Wake up, Rise, Shine, in other words, Eat, Bathe, Forsake]

Inhalación [Inhalation / breathing, exposure time is important, on that vacation the plane circling for an hour unable to land, purgatorial teal of the Pacific and not a pocket of rough air to be found, the pilot's dulcet crackled over the loudspeaker, We may be able to descend but never fly this vessel again, I was breathing short crisp breaths between my legs, and happy to be alive later on we ran naked, head-first into the raging sea Take us back! only later learning of the trench however many thousands of units deep right offshore, the boats losing their anchors, down, down, down]

Contacto con la piel [Skin contact, too easy, dangers are obvious, do whatever you can to get to out of your skin, run until your gums bleed or scratch at the bite, he says Can you really say you're from this country if you haven't had dengue, if you haven't washed a window with a dry cloth, stolen bread, stuck your hands into a bucket of cement or food and felt it all around and mixed it all up like your life and loves depended on it]

Contacto con los ojos [Contact with the eyes, eye contact, visual contact, What beautiful pupils he said once When dilated, Take care of yourself, Remember to drink water, Walk all you want, Imagine the view from up there, Take your pepper spray, Get big and back away from the bear, Read on what to do in the case of a panther, Love, Do you ever wonder what if this were all happening somewhere else?]

Ingestión [Ingestion, to swallow, Is that the name of a bird he asks, acceptance, there are two sides to everything, the table, the couch, the bed, the garden, the leaf, the stone, it's too easy, you name it, everything has at least two sides, Is this a mathematical argument he asks, No, I'd argue anything except math with you]

Indicaciones adicionales [Further indications, none]

ISLA ESPÍRITU SANTO

Forty dollars takes one onto the open sea but we think in pesos and *mares abiertos*;
  that's why

the drunk boater makes sense to me; I want him and his empty blue beer box for
  myself.

We are many leagues deep. A whale flashes us her heart. A tourist is grazed up by
  medusas.

How dare we serve ourselves fish from a cooler. How dare we get drunk. This
  adorable ocean

would suck us down in fewer than two thoughts. Beneath the surface, my husband's
  hand is a star,

but we'd wanted more; to chase exotic creatures into coves and risk being speared
  through the heart.

We wanted the orca. How sad, says the innkeeper, to watch a mother teach her
  young to hunt

other young. But maybe baby that's just life. In our tiny room, in its vacuum
  shower, I work bar soap

into my new husband's hair. Indeed, he is a very new husband. How sad, says the
  innkeeper, about

the girl who collided with an arcing whale and died but also she had it coming. My
    new husband

and I tend to agree. Does the innkeeper want us for herself? She parts us papaya
    before we wake

which means she does. How nice it will be to jilt her for each other. A tail slap, a
    round leap; pack up;

we still have a mating game. The island unhooks and lodges itself in our brains
    though once we go

we hardly ever check in on it. On the ride out our windshield smacks dead a bird
    and with our weak

smiles and bulbous tears we're saying how glad we are to be hunters.

BACTERIA

In the gut and the garden and the ways I am trying to keep others alive.
Triple-washed greens and never water from the tap
of the lake of dinghies, of snakes leeching bathers.
One thing I admire about humanity is our resistance to civilization.
Sometimes it is enough to be breasted and keen.

QUIZ: HOW PATIENT ARE YOU?

Did you know that the term "patience" comes from the Latin "patientia" meaning submission, indulgence and leniency? What about the word's relationship to submission to lust? Not to be too hard on you, but the first, second and third times you were assaulted, you chalked it up to lust. Can you imagine? Patience for the man who steals your keys ands seals the mouth of winter. Patience for the man who fills your tub and drowns the month of June. Patience for the man who gives you poison and kills the night in its sleep. Fine, then; you were once the picture of patience. But, how patient are you now? What patience do you have for your olive green mugs being stored with your forest green mugs? What patience do you have for your husband's mis-makings of the bed and the unbearable beauty of his flagrant impatience in the haphazard scatter of pillows? It is practically good art. How patient are you with your saplings; isn't it you who is always urging the fruit to grow? Please. You want a good lime, but you'll forget to pick it ripe and it will drop. How patient are you with the life cycle? It has been five years, and you are still waiting for your body to tell you what to do with it. Are you patient enough to make a lineage? To give children meaningful names? Will you ever finish the Russian novels? The names! Woman: don't divert. Are you patient enough to be selfless? That is, to cut your husband's hair without watching the time but instead feeling the time as a curled lock? To ease oil into his skin, across the tract of his back? Can you bathe the baby as many times as need be? Can you stare down the figure of the amount of times you'll wash these floors and not give up on life? Can you sum the miles in your legs? The growths and trims of a cuticle? Can you let just one day unlatch itself and leave without trying to reel it back in to be all yours? Can you allow the other to be all his and watch him open, wilt, drop, open, wilt, drop for all of time? Woman: are you patient? We'll calculate your result.

Medios de extinción [Extinguishing methods / Extinction methods, Whatever you do do not leave do not come back do not go out do not stay here do not sleep upstairs do not sleep on the couch do not drive so slowly do not be reckless do not cry do not stop talking do not show so much emotion do not leave the water boiling do not let the gas run out of the stove come on we could die in our sleep]

Peligros especiales [Special dangers / first-rate dangers / exceptional dangers / certain dangers / appropriate dangers / exclusive dangers / rich dangers / poor dangers / in-sickness dangers / in-health dangers / individual dangers / limited dangers / memorable dangers / vacation dangers / peculiar dangers / god dangers / secular dangers / proper dangers / rude dangers / rare dangers / one-in-a-million dangers / smashing dangers / fusion dangers / red-letter dangers / written-word dangers / spoken-word dangers / unspoken dangers / unreal dangers / fictional dangers / festive dangers / the-whole-family-is-here dangers / everyone-is-here-for-you dangers / no-one-is-there-for-you dangers / select dangers / self-selected dangers / uncommon dangers / remediless dangers / reserved dangers / just-for-you dangers / it's-all-for-you dangers, and in the time I've taken to name the dangers, the dangers have gone out to hide and the word is trembling and makes a different face and sound]

Consejos [Advice / consultation / What is better? A new home or a new plot? This country? That country? New shoes or repaired shoes? Elocution or reticence? Asking for permission or forgiveness? Writing it down or making a mental note? Out of mercy, I want to know what's in his head. What are you thinking? Is it trite to ask Is this how to love you? Is this fit okay? Is the fabric nice? How was your day? Did you come? What does it feel like for you when I breathe up the fringe on your neck? When I pat you back down to sleep when you've yelled out from your dream God! or Ghost!]

ON HAVING CHILDREN

What I don't want? I think I know:
I don't want to become tenuous again, right when
I'd gotten things down, when I could ride

the highway without turning into a bag of bones, right
when I could catapult at 40,000 feet without
incinerating and could watch the woman in the first seat

of the plane bounce up to shuffle her bags and say to myself
she knows she'll never die, what children she'll have—
But, I don't want a world of ladders, of high windows,

of a pill I dropped. Of our need. Our desire for silence. For clean
and hard concrete and adult television. Yet, here I am
with my sister and her infant on linoleum in her

house of dangers and she is the calmest I've ever seen anyone—
what it must be to know your body did more than simply survive.
We are dressing up baby, decorating baby's crown with candy—

children in a game we've made from found objects,
plotting, you be the this and I'll be the that and we'll roll for who
shoves all the pieces back into the box. What do we win? Here,

with her newborn murmuring beside the clawfoot tub, she says
if anything ever happens to me, and I won't even let her say it.

ILLNESS

The tanker idles while the driver gets inside.
The woman of the house next door has her wig on today.
She prescripts lingering, directs boots to trudge all over the scene.
Call the curtain down. I am nostalgic already for incandescent light.
I still only want to die in this world.

Conv. # THE BOILER

Wife & Husband

Is the boiler on   is it off   did you turn the nob to pilot isn't it a bit luxurious
to wash your hands in hot water   what if we burn down the house oh well let's
keep moving   it's not like we can never leave   so I can see now   how a boiler
could tear even a solid couple apart   the secret blue flame heating even
the garden hose   all so one can repose under the piping tap   it's profane
that moment of heat more delectable than an entire marriage of delicacies   I'll be
honest   my desire is for that blazing ring   all day working consuming gorging
on the shares of nature   because I am the center of my universe and what good
am I to anyone else without even a warm hand for work

MAL DE DEBARQUEMENT

I cannot want for my husband's body and his body cannot for mine.
Instead I use the bed for well-being, for bad-being, for my poor little self.

I tilt my head 45 degrees, then 90—and on one side, I am looking straight at him,
and it is tender and it is frail and above all too much. I can get out of bed
on one side

and be alone, or on the other, and trespass his body, traverse his body to do so.
I am buoyed between the word in my right ear and the one in my left.

Indefinitely on the swell, I am, maybe, then again, on the crest.
I get a message out to him: *if this makes any sense to you, pull me out; shore
me up.*

Precauciones personales [Personal precautions, none]

Precauciones ambientales [Environmental precautions, concern for your
surroundings, I say to myself Self, Re-Write the Ending! I'm shutting off the drip,
cutting the flame, putting disinfectant in the water, tying back my hair before I
cook, I am making meals for four just in case he and I have double the hunger than
usual, in Sunday's stupor we play Apocalypse, a very real game, We'll need sacks of
dried beans, peas, honey bees, water filtration, solar, a seed bank, paint or a hobby
for happiness, That's a good one! You'd survive! No, you'd survive! Re-write the
ending: we win, we win, we win]

Contención y limpieza [Containment and cleanup, let's go for a new tree, spend the
afternoon at the nursery inquiring into the rituals of each plant, high as kites in our
Sunday sweats, all the life here! What if we fill in the roof with soil and trellises,
Let's do it, Careful now, Balance the ladder, Find a low center of gravity, Like an
animal, Crawl to me, What if we plant this here, Where will it hang down to in
a year?]

41

THE MEN: PART 1

One day the men arrive to the lot next door. They lean their shovels, picks, and trowels against our outer wall, and I feel it like a poke to my breastbone or a knuckle tap to my skull. The first thing I say to them after I greet them is if they will be ruining our wall to which they respond no but that they will be building another wall against it. I ask them if they will leave a human-wide space. For maintenance. No.

The sound of the shovel is one of the most calming there is. Some people listen to recordings of waves, but I would choose one of a shovel filling itself with moderate mouthfuls of loosely packed dirt. The shovel is calming because it represents work. It is calming because it has a capacity and meter. It is calming because it is often and unpredictably imperfect, striking a stone or a pipe. The shovel allows itself to err and move on.

The oldest of the men starts digging. He works until the batteries in his radio drain out and the sun gets too high and brazen. Of the group, he is the strongest and the most alive and the least likely to die, and it crosses my mind that he could dig steady under and up into my house. But he digs a perfectly restrained rectangle, a resting place for plumbing or the Internet. It is all part of the plan on the long scroll. The men squint at it in the unmitigated light.

When the men go home for the day or before they arrive in the morning, I walk past the site. I think how, in my life, I have never been inside of the earth. I could lower myself into the ditch to frighten a passerby, get a new point of view, participate in an uncomplicated metaphor. How calming. But at any given moment the men could arrive with their shovels and continue to work around me. Imagine the embarrassment. At any given moment we could get an earthquake. Or a flood. It's always wise, I think, to consider the proximity of ruin.

The men do not come every day and there is no pattern to their comings and goings. When they are gone, I do not miss them, but when they return and I hear the swoosh of their shovels, I realize that I had missed them after all and wish they'd at least be consistent. Occasionally, they lose control of a downswing and chip our concrete. I knew they were lying about our wall. That's why the last thing I said to them was ok and very well, so that they'd know they aren't hurting me or what I've built here and that I love work as they love work and am on the other side of it all day swooping, plunging, clanging, in my own way.

INTERROGATION:

You are good. No. Are you? As in
on the other side of evil. Yes, you are short-nailed
and sheared, mispacked and rude; blood stains
your gums and you have stones jangling
in your joints. When you were young,
lovers would open their downy lives for you.
When you were young, you were a landscape unto itself.

THE FRIEND

There are two ways to die from lightning.
One. It gets your whole house.
Two. It gets only you.

This is what the friend tells me
as we walk the sidewalk, or
maybe the friend tells me in a

sidewalked dream. Maybe the friend
tells me when she descends upon the television
as an on-screen angel. It doesn't matter how I remember;

the friend believes in the apocalypse,
and I cannot. Yet—when the rods of lightning
poke at my bitty bit of land, I think of the friend

and pray though I know prayers turn
to stone and sit for years in the same place.
Jagged oaths dive down the sky—sideways

mouths that go in for lie. The friend said
she knew a whole family consumed by lightning. Why
is it that I believe her? The sky groans

and pawns of hail split the avenue and cabdrivers
stall and smoke. The friend in her walls
and I in mine, both considering the clawing of light,

how it will take everything a woman has.
Yet, my breathing is more guttural than
that of eternal life and my sweat is as vital as ever.

FIDELITY
Wife & Husband

Husband these are my legs sinewed & strong my back that never sags no matter
     the fat I carry once
when I was a girl in school a teacher said to us humans are ugly animals ask a
     team of humans to run
across a field & it is nothing compared to the beauty of a sprinting harras
     I suppose I thought
the teacher had a point husband who could want me husband why is this what
     has stayed with me
husband I am a broken record with this but did you know that once I fell for a
     man who'd whistle
through the door fresh in from his lover's rounded thighs he'd say now just what
     kind of man
do you think I am and if I spooked he'd say woman you are an unloveable beast
     husband I am how I
am I don't mean to dream you cold in bed saying you're not sure that I that you
     don't know if you want that maybe
you should have gone for a numinous human who knew how to lighten a mood

AFTER THE ASSASSINATIONS

I hear a woman say that it's terrible, but
one gets much more done when the rest are afraid to go out.
At every stand, sappy pineapple and vibrant flank on the hook.
I know she's good, so I know what she means.
Part of grieving is keeping everyone fed.

TERMINAL

There is a second on the night bus from here to there
when you are released from your life and
become a gum in the soft mouth of a small,
yellow light. In life, you have failed and
thank the gods, the big gods, you have because
now you are a kernel, a single woo of wind,
a tender needle, a knot in the net;
you are a satin-lined death. You are all of
the love anyone could ever need, and your life, in all of
the ways it is wrong for you, is out there like the terminal:
tiled, fluorescent, entropic. Necessitous and starved,
it is for you who always returns.

Precauciones para un manejo y almacenamiento seguro [precautions for safe
handling, safekeeping, Mama told me you better—forget the rest, I keep my shirts
in an envelope fold, I keep my socks in a ball, I keep my hair in a tiny knot, I keep
plates clean and days dull, I am as dull as the dishwater, I keep my chest high and
eyes low, sometimes I raise my voice and yell Do you desire me and he whispers It's
always been you or There's never a lull]

Usos específicos [specific uses, green plate is to silver spoon as white mug is to blue
coaster, gray floor is to white bed as orange blanket is to orange tree, sarape is to
someone's grandfather as talking about boys' eyes is to getting a life lesson from
my father (eyes don't make it real!), words are to notebook as fruit wrapper is to
rined fruit, I am to you as you are to me, setting a trap is to you as releasing a trap
is to me, two toothbrushes murmuring over our respective teeth another night is to
marriage as the price of gold is to the price of gold]

THE MEN: PART 2

While I wait for the boiler to heat the tank for a scalding shower in the middle of summer, I watch the men fill buckets, hoist them, and send them up the pulley. The summer of the subtropics is unreliable and cold in a flash. Yesterday, we had four feet of ice. This is not magical realism though we gorge ourselves on that too. This is the end of the world.

It is a dear thing to make a wall. How thick and how sturdy you make it is directly correlated to how much you care about other people. Some of the neighbors' houses share a wall; one wall leans on another, and leaning is directly correlated to danger. I think I would know what to say if a wall were to lean on mine. I would know how to make the men care about me.

Like I said, it's dear. Tender. It takes a certain amount of empathy to measure and assure ten centimeters of girth to numb sound or withstand or make sure one feels alone when one needs to feel alone. Is it a kitchen wall? Is the future children or adults? Among the men, at least one must be a prophet, and I think I'll share with him how I had always believed that at the end of the world people would come together like in the movies. Not symbolically but literally. Families living together under one roof and stocking cans. Wearing tool belts and sharpening knives by fires. Everyone would be able to make fire.

How softhearted, concrete's process. Stirring water into a fine mix of stone. Neither too little or too much. Then, it's with the hands, rounded hands like hands on shoulders. Reassurance. Providence. Mothering. The sun is out. A storm from the next county can be heard.

I wonder if the men see me. A face behind a mosquito screen. If they think I'm an apparition. There is no sadness in their work today so I must be nothing to them. Like when I am working well and forget to eat my apple. The refrigerator churns and the boiler hisses; water scurries up the wall. When the men break for lunch I'm so lonely I think I'll fix a plate and go out there. I'd always believed that at the end of the world I wouldn't be afraid of men, that we'd get each other—time being of the essence and all.

But, I take my shower and heat bread and dig my teeth in and think about how to end a poem when it's on a pulley and I'm not sure how high the wall should be or if it should be or why I started it in the first place. And because this is the end of the world, I think how I could let it go, all of it: the pulley, the thought, the care. That is—I could not write, or empathize, or pilot the flame, or only eat my share.

Conv. **SHOVELING AT NIGHT**

Wife to Self

I say to myself   go to the window   see what's not there   the shovelers asleep and
the shovels in other towns crane your neck   see further now break your body
strain   good girl   focus   quiet now   turn around   look inward
no look close   now do you see the source   your husband's breathing
ragged   in/in   out/out   stop   did you hear that   he's hit a stone

QUIZ: HOW RESIGNED ARE YOU?

This is a good one. Give up, abandon, relinquish, cancel, give back, give up. Give a sign. That said, to what extent are you resigned? The implications of this question may be painful: if you reach out to keep someone from falling down a flight of stairs and that person still falls, is this your fault? We think you'd say yes, but that doesn't make you a better person. After all, the body still falls. The body can still break. When your husband's mind is a mess of exposed wires, what in the name of God do you do? When your husband is the jester in the room, the life of the party, can you let him have it? Could you muster a laugh? What was it he once loved so much? Watching a pathetic, little river rip with force? Finding the most wild weed and declaring it as pretty as a houseplant? Picking up opal from the forest floor as if it were rare? Losing time? Willingly, blissfully blowing through time. Not watching one's words. Talking with a full mouth. Driving on a patched flat. Counting the ringing shots in the night from inside the sturdy house. So lucky you were, you didn't even wonder if you'd ever have to prevent disaster. So lucky you were. Can he still feel it? Can you?

DAMNED

Isn't it what we are always doing? Loosening up our ties to one another, lifting up
our skirts? The hunter of my dream fires rounds at the dark and my legs go soft
sprinting away up a mulched path. This interminable city, molten and drowned.
The husband of my dream convinces me down into the metro, the train darting blind
on rubber wheels. The earth shakes; the self of my dream cuts a dead inch
from her hair without a mirror, awake looks for evidence of the clean-sheared
line, of growth to a bruise, a vein in the wall. She checks between her thighs
and into the reaches of her mind. Who's there, she says.

GASOLINE RATIONS

If the sun ran on a combustion engine, then this would be rich;
crude irony. Helios and the government—conspiring.
Whatever. Down here we're witness to humanity:
dog eat dog eat dog in the equatorial heat.
I'm too desirous to wait my turn.
My fantasy, still, is to die from the inside out.

Controles de exposición [exposure controls]:

A. Protección para los ojos [eye protection: see everything, the scratch across the table and the shard of glass you missed while sweeping, sweep the hills for fire and sweep the hills for bright birds, pan the ocean for contamination and for new species of fish in a flap of coral, if you're always looking you'll never miss something, like that time he and I went swimming in the reserve and I screamed out for him when I saw the sand and that the sand had eyes and then wings and the monstrous ray flapped me back to shore to drip and huddle and spit into my towel and say I want nothing to do with water anymore]

B. Protección para la piel [skin protection: try to think about what you want as little as possible unless you can have it, like how I don't think about putting my ankles up by his neck, our two bodies on the porch when there's not a soul around unless he's close enough for me to put my ankles up by his neck and unless I can get all the souls off our porch]

C. Protección para la boca [mouth protection: don't bring that language you got from outside into this house, don't come in saying What a day or You'll never believe what happened, don't come in here using words I don't know or we didn't invent, Don't cough into the air, Don't cry for mama, Don't snore, Don't let the neighbor hear you though we can hear the neighbor, hysterical—this a good talking point—Is he devastated by loss or glad that someone's gone?]

D. Protección para los pulmones [lung protection: only take what you need, and by God put on your own mask before assisting others, actually do not take this last piece of advice, it is classically bad, put your masks on at the same time, nod to each other, wink, give a little look like an eye that wants to say something from across the room at a party What dumb politics What bad art What silly friends If we're going down, then, at least we're going down together]

54

PRAYER

When my mother goes, then,
   bring on the super volcano. I wouldn't

even have time to feel bad for the rest
   of humanity, for once, this time,

not time to dwell on the knots in the floor, what
   with the five-thousand-degree billow decimating

us or —because in the end it depends on
   the wind—our going slow with the flora

trapped under the brume, the bleared sun
   struggling to make a a difference anymore.

I feel bad even writing this.
   I feel bad even thinking this. As if

this thought will be the pin in the crater
   like those scientists want to be, only their attempt

would be preventative and I'd get it all wrong.
   I feel so bad I could cry.

See, when I lived on earth
   I appreciated a good crane, a bloom

fanning in yellow and orange shrapnel.
   How I wished to see, just once, god, any god,

perched in a tree. How it hurt to live on earth,
   to feel my poor face change night after night

into that of a new woman and another to watch
   myself have to learn itself time and time again—

time again   that was a thing I used to say
   on earth   how I used attempt prayer from

time to time   Dear God don't ever let my mother—
   nights awake wrapped in the nebula of

my body—ending with and God,
   I've decided, that the super volcano, no.

Conv. **GOING OUT**

Wife & Husband

Now You do know that if I wanted to I could go out right now and find someone
        else to love me
the neighbor with the new Volvo a hipster with a beautiful dog the lonely man
        who summons
a bus of musicians to play a ballad for him You do know I could go out on this
        walk and never
come back that the hills would take me that a river would that somewhere
        womankind
with a full house would even say fine come in and feed me but You and this is
        the problem
even the perimeter of our house loves You that neighbor combs his hair for You
        the office
perfumes and preens for You it's grotesque Your beauty to be with You is to
        love an echo
to want to gulp down glasses of sound

INTERROGATION:

There you are. Up the hill. One more bend
and you'll turn back. You'll come up on a bridge and mile marker
and be disappointed. You like being the only sign
of life. Don't you? Up the hill your face can be chapped,
your cheeks swelled and everything uncomely. You
can be ugly as sin. Those rings around your eyes!
How many suitors would have left you for dead
if you hadn't known how to pluck the night.

HOJA DE DATOS DE SEGURIDAD [SAFETY DATA SHEET]
SECCIÓN 8 [SECTION 8]
INFORMACIÓN TOXICOLÓGICA [TOXICOLOGICAL INFORMATION] [ALT.:
IMMINENCE]

Efectos toxicológicos, general [Overview of toxicological effects, personal, the
locked teeth of combs in a drawer, in the heat the door is too wide for the jamb,
in the rain the paint drags down the wall, all the tiny purple limbs of the lavender
have the rest of the garden in a chokehold, but I do what I can, when the sink is
full of soap, I leave the graters, blades, peelers, to one side to protect his soft hands,
when the knives need sharpening I sharpen them with other knives, when his
saplings need watering I try to call down the rain]

Supuesto práctico [Case study]

Efecto toxicológico potencial [Potential toxicological effect]

Parámetro [Parameter]: Distance

Ruta de exposición [Exposure route]: I drove across a country, I got my kicks, I
lost my wits in the wind fields of the panhandle and got them back in Monument
Valley, by the time I reached the blazing disturbance of the Red Rocks I was alive,
I rolled down the window, I hung out my hand, I sang a folk song over and over
until dizzy and a drunk driver almost killed me, I shook, my mind wandered, I
thought How does food get all the way out here, I received an amber alert, I passed
up hitchhiking families, I had a woman flag me down, I punctured a tire, I parked
in a canyon, I watched the military planes round, *Lord I swore I would never miss a
man* until I was driving across the wasteland, peaks growing but never nearing and I
screamed for him and was not crazy because no one would ever hear me]

Dosis efectiva [Effective dose, places I may have died alone]: 38.3670° N, 111.2615°
W; 32°15′52″N, 100°20′39″W; 42.3063° N, 113.3692° W; 46°41′47.7″N, 117°00′28.8″W

Resultado [Outcome]: What idiocy to choose a life alone

EVE OF THE RAIN SEASON

It's the last night of heat, of annihilation. This year
our violence went for the head. An amber beam
of drought stretching no *across a callous neck. Tomorrow,*
I will plaster the wall where I bored the hole too high to hang
a print that reads apocatastasis. *This repair could feel for me*
like what the ajolote must feel upon regenerating its own brain.
What a kingdom: animalia. We don't deserve it.

TRÁMITE

At the office, I am assigned the wrong husband.
The same five names as another equals an easy mistake.
A concrete-colored lizard distracts itself down
a concrete-colored wall outside the window where
I am to file to my complaint. It will take time.

Meantime. The new husband is like the old husband
in the way a plot is the same once the vegetation's
been lopped off it. Understand that neither
he nor I are necessarily the vegetation or the lot.
New husband has a different hairline. Unfamiliar dampness.
He laughs along with the laugh track. Insists on boxed milk.

I've never asked New what he does. It doesn't matter.
New, I know, has an extramarital lover. She is like me
in the way a plot is the same once a structure
has been built on it. Understand that neither
she nor I are necessarily the structure or the lot.
It's just a dimensional difference. Lover

wears my earrings, wears my robe.
When New and Lover kiss they open their
mouths as wide as heads. Lover and New make
a video and leave it around. I watch
until a hand comes over the camera and
cuts the sex. It was, I imagine, like a glass bulb.

I do not love my replacement husband
and he does not love me. Saying it simple is better
because I can't access all the mind I'd want to.
I escalate my complaint at the window.
On that wall, it is either a trick lizard or lost.

What I would give, now, for my old husband.
For his wan whistling and his straight, long calves
What I would give for his tantrums and declarations.
Common ground. Uncommon ground. Two grounds
that are ours the way one's home in one season is
the same enough as it is in another. Uncanny grounds.

What would you give, asks the official, following suit.
If I'd be willing to give, she'll shuffle the names.

If she may—I might've deserved this. The way I confuse
streets in a storm, when the lines are scrubbed and the signs felled.
She's not wrong. The official is like me in the way one person
is like another person, just with different DNA.

It takes years but I get my original husband back. So rare,
we have the government over for dinner. Original and I,
together, clear and wash the plates. When our guests are gone,
we're alone in our walls and the world rages improbable
in the heads of fauna and the cells of flora. This means,
I think, that love is dubious at best.

                    No matter.
I run my hands along Original's calves.

SAN SEBASTIÁN

It may have been one of the times we died, only to come right back. Maybe we
rolled

the car and were reborn in the woods without a clue. At least I hope death is like
this:

a town with just two restaurants. What a steady fire I make against the night.
What a good rock he

chooses to stave off wild dogs. We're going to survive every life, he & I. We walk 50
kilometers

for pleasure, and after the first third he thinks he's dying, this time of mal de altura,

and because in this kind of town you can, we find a shrine and get his sugar up at
the hem

of the Virgin. If there is an afterlife, may it be a place where you can still get sick
from

doing dumb things like climbing too high too fast. He and I need to feel like we
survived;

it means something to him that I nod and say let's get down from here when the
men charge

up the hill in their hideous trucks. Since I think we may be dead, I let him tell the
story

of his brother's bite again. The scar that moved up the leg as he grew until it was a
      notch

for lovers to score. How neither ground glass nor rat poison would kill the dog.
      Good

on the dog; may the afterlife bite. The more I say, the more I realize I'm not fit to
      die, or be

anywhere but San Sebastián on my birthday, pushing our bodies to the edge, telling
      him

to pin my hands to the bed behind my head because with that kind of trust he & I
      will live forever.

Reactividad [Reactivity]: The product is stable.

Estabilidad química [Chemical stability]: The product is stable, the product is stable, Repeat after me, the product is stable.

Condiciones a evitar [Conditions to be avoided]: Where have we not been? In my mind he runs his hand over moss, he scoops a worm into his palm, he cups a wild fish, he pets the dog, he pats his own hair down under his hat, he lifts the baby, he snaps a bud, he soaps his back, he folds the blanket, he presses his pen, he maneuvers the car, he squares up his fingers, he frames the light, he takes food in, he slides the screen, he shutters the rain, he pushes a button, he turns it on, he puts it in drive, he shifts to reverse, he aligns the corners, he cuts his nails, he grips the handles, he reaches the ground, he breaks his fall, he applauds, clap clap, this is the entire universe, where have we not been?

Materiales incompatibles [Incompatible materials]: The material is compatible.

Descomposición peligrosa [Hazardous decomposition]: The material is compatible, the material is compatible, Repeat after me, the material is compatible. Note: But what do compatible materials and decomposition have to do with one another? Revisit. One and another: two words holding each other up. Now, shaking the ladder.

THE MEN: PART 3

Once they had the four walls up, the men started building a secret world inside them. It's the only thing they could have been doing in there for all that time. Now, with a tarp over the entrance, the only way to see their world would be to trespass.

On a Sunday morning, I am the only one up in the neighborhood. I know I shouldn't be proud of this but I am. Everything, though it isn't much, is mine: the energy plant, the mopey saplings, the blue plastic bubbles stretched over the pool. This is more than what I usually have and I am powerful. I am invisible like the children who stay out late on the basketball court learning to curse, believing no one can hear them through the chain-link.

When I was a child my father and I would enter the near-finished homes of new subdivisions. It wasn't breaking and entering because these houses belonged to the man and not to actual people and anyways locks hadn't been put on the doors. Every time, I wanted to move. Imagine the liberation a new pantry could bring. One of the houses at the top of a hill had an observation tower and two staircases. With two staircases the two halves of our family could circulate the house without ever meeting.

One Sunday morning, I try the door of a near-finished house two streets down. This is the warm-up for entering the secret world. From the window, I can see that this house is just a house. There is nothing secret, not even its cabinets seem to hold anything close. Anyways the door is bolted. There is a single plastic chair; surely it has been passed from place to place.

There was only one time I didn't want to move. The house, which had a backyard that sloped treacherously towards woods like the woods where my sister got Lyme, was next door to the house of the prettiest girl in school. No good for a pool, my father said. I thought of the girl's mother's hands. Her rings. We were going to get caught by that girl's mother, and she'd look at us the way she looked at me the time I dropped my sister off to play. Like she had more time than my mother and only she could know the worth of time.

The Sunday I entered the secret world I got out of bed so stealthily my husband didn't stir, and I ate my morning meal in silence. I wouldn't have to go far. The world was right next door. All I had to do was pull back the tarp and let myself in, and I did. The house was like any: four walls, partitions, windows. But, at the same time, the house was different enough from mine for me to know that this is what it felt like to be opposite myself. I have a deep wrinkle I knew nothing about. My mouth leans a way when I talk and another when I smile. My husband's desperation is loneliness and his loneliness is not mine. The name he calls in his sleep is of a mother he longed to have.

Down off the dirt road a few miles from where we lived was the house my father would have bought if he could have. A modern ranch with floor-to-ceiling windows behind which was his secret world. We never snuck in; it was never uninhabited; no one ever gave it up. But in there was a telescope, for sure. Aerodynamic bicycle wheels and a mother who knew how to ride. A dog that slept inside. Rare vegetables. Little girls who didn't have fever or trouble. Icons blessed in myrrh. If I had to say. In there was man with a direct line to God.

QUIZ: HOW ENDURING ARE YOU?

There is a lot to consider here. Endurance in terms of strength. Endurance in terms of virility. Endurance in terms of mortality. Continued existence in time. Related to fortitudinous and firmness. You once survived something big. Pulled the stem of a root stuck hard in the ground. Cured the cut of a nailhead in your thigh. You made ends meet. You managed to survive yourself. You managed. Let's leave it at that. You even, at times, let yourself lose your head. Here's something we're sure you're tired of not being able to say: you have loved. And, now the question: for how long? What if we count the years left in your knees, in your head, in your organs and take an average? What about when you're gone? What if it's worse? What if it's not clean-cut? Before you travel you whisper a sentence into your husband's ear you never thought you'd be able to form with so few modifiers and addenda. You see that it makes him feel something within the scope of this micro-ending. What will you most want when it's really over? To observe? To watch your husband tidy the house in innocence and vigor, entraining his body to a thought repeating deep and far in his head? Or something more tender—watching him reheat a meal or shift his lips to the mirror? How do we know you'll die first? We don't, but we think that booming drum of sadness suits you. That you could entrain to that long, heavy note; good work. Do we know how it ends? We do. But, we can't say. We know you're trying to write into the blank and that you keep running over your own words. Obliterating the lines is so much cleaner. What is it that you struggle so much to know, and why do you want to know it?

UNDESIRABLE THOUGHTS

In the mine of my husband's head a canary descends and he sends another after it and so on. If I didn't intimately understand, I'd shake him awake, say someday your body will be as broad as a god's and I'll have hair so thick and long I won't know what to do with it.

Persistencia y degradabilidad [Persistence and degradability]: You can have it all. What's done is done. No sense crying over the milk that's spilled. God forgives. God is dead. I will survive. You can make it if you try. Blood runs thick. Come hell or high water. Get your head right. Don't throw out your darlings.

Potential acumulativo [Accumulative potential / potential of accumulation]: Hope springs eternal in the human beast. Take the money and run. The past is the past. You can have it all. Thicker than water, the whistling woman. A whistling woman and a crowing hen are neither fit for God nor men. A silent woman and a silent hen are no use to man or beast.

Tratamiento de desechos [Processes of undoing]: Do not despair. You can get it all. A country, a god, a man, some love.

Conv. **THE LOCK**

Wife, Husband, Therapist

We didn't used to have a lock because who would steal from us but when they did
     come they left
their flashlight on the dresser   when they did come the neighbors said good
     evening   suits and leather
when they did come they strangled a dog and exited through the roof   they took
     our cigar box of history
when they did come they missed the stash in the drawer   they experienced ecstasy
     against our door
we stayed up that night   and   when they did come again they brought a lunatic to
     beat us as if we
were someone else   left us a pepper bush as an apology   but how scared we became
     how that of all things
ruined it for us   how I'm a fiend and he's a burier   but smart we are   do you know
     what we did
we got the best lock money can buy in the state of Jalisco

MANZANILLA DE LA PAZ

We do know God. An eared quetzal on a devoniana pine of least concern

about three kilometers down. Last night I looked up what other people were
    looking up

on the internet: the etymology of God. It's what you'd expect. A red belly, an
    iridescent tuft.

We squealed. Knowing the quetzal has brought us closer. I undo two buttons on my
    husband's work shirt

and am awash for the first time years; why is it we don't consider enough the
    miracle

of the body, the opus of organs intoning? Should this be allowed? My heavy hand on
    his breastbone

in peacemaking? The surge of his circulatory system on a divine metronome. I
    looked it up:

wonder. It's what you'd expect. It was an Orthodox monk who told me to not take
    creation literally,

that it involved all of time, even today. His humanness is improving with the tick

of the pendulum. But, this human here between beats is something to behold;

I'll need to remember him: his perch, his airfoil, the span of his wings.

AFTERLIVING, AN APPENDIX

The longer I keep the house shut, the more it becomes clear to me that this is the afterlife.
> First, the very obvious bird of paradise. Secondly, the geographically incongruent light.

So this is it. A mug two shades lighter than I remember and new angles on the bed corners.
> A mouth that no longer leans anywhere. A deep inking of the letters. If I'm being honest:

does the water taste that much better? Is it that much more fun to open my legs in the
> middle of the afternoon when I should be working? What, without thirst or work?

Do I finally get it: eternity? The everlasting party—immortal friends and all-time favorite
> hits coming in clearer on the best audio system souls can buy—everyone flopping down on divans

and crying sweet, sweet tears for our past lives? Emptying our chests without the headache?
> And no morning rings around the eyes. Didn't someone love me once for my rings, back there

in the before? There, I hungered and forged. Here, a deity drops me a cookie. Good girl.
> Good being. Good soul. The deity reminds me of what I do not miss: milk, beestings, mold.

Besides. There's no going back. I stare down the thick, whole fronds of the garden beyond the living room window. Not a hail-stain. Not a wormhole. I used to hoist my body up

and out of the chair to yank a nasty weed. Got pleasure from watching the dirt rinse out of my nails
> and taint the basin. Pleasure. Pleasure! Do you remember the good old fix of it:

hankerings and results? The construction of one's decisiveness—I like this, not that. I like not
> the fresh coat of paint. I like not my face. I like to wait on line and be told

today's not my day and have to use charm to get my way. I think we all
        get it: I miss playing god. Making someone feel something. Whittling
        matter down into a shape—

something like personality or affection, a string of words or a hot meal. And
everything
        only to the degree that I could I make it and say that it was good.

La información proporcionada en esta hoja de datos de seguridad the information provided in this safety data sheet *es correcta a nuestro leal saber y entender* is correct insofar as we can see *la información proporcionada está diseñada solo como guía* this information is solely intended as a guide *y no se considera una garantía de calidad* and is not considered a guarantee of quality *la información se relaciona solo con el material específico designado y puede no ser válida para dicho material* the information is solely related to the Specific Designated Material and may not be valid for even said material *cuando éste sea usado en combinación con cualquier otro material* when said material is taken in conjunction with any other material *a menos que se especifique en el texto* you must follow the text *no somos responsables de ninguna pérdida o daño* losses and damages are up to you *por el uso del producto en aplicaciones para las cuales no fue diseñado* always you can re-write the ending *y por condiciones de uso contrarias* always you can re-enter *a las recomendaciones de esta hoja de datos* always you can cover your eyes ears mouth *versiones previas ya no son válidas* see no hear no speak no *versiones previas ya no son válidas* you cannot believe everything even if sworn *pero siempre puedes regresar al inicio*

74

O

GARDEN

I wanted right now to write a poem that had exuberance in it   a poem about
      younger people doing things like throwing their whole lives
into the orbit of sex but my husband is naming the potential
      deaths of the garden's plants using
even the Latin names   he's reading the encyclopedia instead of working again
      and I don't have the energy for it
reading or encyclopedias   work or death   if I'm headed for anything so be it
      today I had the first thought
I actually believed about dying young   I could see it and it was like any other time
      I've let something go because
I needed something else more and first and now I know that when they say
      live fast and die young
they also don't mean so young just too young to die   my husband says
      the *Philodendron selloum* may burn
and the *Sedum Morganianum* may drown but that the *Monstera* is smart
      and knows where to put its roots
and look for *sum umbra*   that is sombra   that is to say
      love and home
I'm sorry I don't have the energy for it but I am trying
      there it is   I've been
to the encyclopedia five times in an hour now and my husband has gone up
      and put on music
in the bedroom and opened the shade   (look how easy it was to open a word)
      just enough for the earth to
ride in and remind us how close we're to it